Sept. 21,

For Roxanna To
share with Skyler
and mommy and
daddy on her
firsT birthday.

With our love!

Grandpa Jon
Grandma Karen

For Kyle and Kirsten,
who have helped me see
through the eyes of a child

AMAZING GRACES

PRAYERS AND POEMS FOR CHILDREN

compiled by JUNE COTNER
illustrated by JAN PALMER

HarperCollinsPublishers

The author would like to extend special thanks to the following critiquers, who helped make this book as special as it is: Colleen Ahern, Patty Ahern, Shannon Ahern, Betty Isgar, Carol-Leah Isgar, Jamie Isgar, Arlene Gay Levine, Cheryl Malcham, Greg Malcham, Jessica Malcham, Timothy Malcham, Kirsten Myrvang, Kyle Myrvang, Margie Cotner Potts, David Reuther, Addie Meyer Sanders, Andrea Spooner, Eric VanAusdal, Sandra VanAusdal, Barbara Younger, and Laura Younger.

Amazing Graces
Compilation © 2001 by June Cotner Graves
Illustrations copyright © 2001 by Jan Palmer
Printed in the U.S.A. All rights reserved.

www.harperchildrens.com

Library of Congress Cataloging-in-Publication Data
Amazing graces : prayers and poems for children / compiled by June Cotner / illustrated by Jan Palmer.—1st ed.
p.   cm.
Includes index.
Summary: A collection of prayers and poems for reading in the morning, at meals, at bedtime, or anytime.
ISBN 0-688-15566-9 — ISBN 0-688-15567-7 (lib. bdg.)
1. Children—Prayer-books and devotions—English. [1. Prayer books and devotions.]   I. Cotner, June, date.   II. Palmer, Jan, ill.
BL625.5 .A48   2001   99-029158
242'.8—dc21   CIP
AC
Typography by Christy Hale
1   2   3   4   5   6   7   8   9   10
❖
First Edition

Contents

A Note about This Book   9

Morning Prayers and Poems   11

Mealtime Prayers and Poems   23

Bedtime Prayers and Poems   33

Anytime Prayers and Poems   43

Title and Author Index   58

A Note about This Book

Children often think praying is only for church, before meals, and when they're kneeling at their bedside. But praying to God doesn't need to be formal or fancy. It can be done anywhere and anytime—morning, noon, and night—as well as at any moment in between. In this book, you'll discover poems and prayers that can be read in the backyard, on a car trip, during playtime, or even in a doctor's waiting room. You'll also find that prayers can take many forms: from a simple sentence ("You and Me Together") to a humorous rhyme ("Peanut Butter Prayer"); from a traditional toast ("To Life!") to the wonderful words of children ("For Goodness' Sake!"); and from the poetry of famous authors to the works of new writers from across the country.

My children and I have had many good talks using these graces as a starting point. Before mealtime, children may choose a favorite grace to read, and afterward, they may want to share why they selected it. At night, parents can browse through the Bedtime section of this book with their children, asking them to share things they like to talk to God about. And during the day, children can read the graces and write poems about a time they felt God helped them; or draw a picture of a special place where they feel close to God; or write their own graces about things they are thankful for.

I believe that children feel closer to God if their ways of talking with God are fresh, simple, and connected to their daily lives. The prayers in this book can inspire such conversations as they celebrate God's role in the common experiences of a child's day, whether it's breakfast cereal or sunshine or a sports game. I encourage all readers of this book to use it as interactively and creatively as possible, for the ability to recognize and appreciate God's wonders surrounding us at each moment is one of the greatest gifts we can give our children.

—June Cotner

MORNING
PRAYERS AND POEMS

Morning

Dear Lord my God,
Good morning!

The rain is falling
to wake the wintry world,
to green the grass,
to bring blossoms to the tree outside my
   window.

The world and I wake up for you.
Alleluia!

MADELEINE L'ENGLE

Morning Has Broken

Morning has broken
Like the first morning,
Blackbird has spoken
Like the first bird.
Praise for the singing!
Praise for the morning!
Praise for them, springing
Fresh from the Word!

Sweet the rain's new fall
Sunlit from heaven,
Like the first dewfall
On the first grass.
Praise for the sweetness
Of the wet garden,
Sprung in completeness
Where his feet pass.

Mine is the sunlight!
Mine is the morning
Born of the one light
Eden saw play!
Praise with elation,
Praise every morning,
God's re-creation
Of the new day!

ELEANOR FARJEON
(1881–1965)

13

Song
(from *Pippa Passes*)

The year's at the spring,
And the day's at the morn;
Morning's at seven;
The hillside's dew-pearled;
The lark's on the wing;
The snail's on the thorn;
God's in his heaven—
All's right with the world.

ROBERT BROWNING
(1812–1889)

Creation

Today I saw the sun come up
and everything was hushed.
To me it seemed pure magic
to watch the world appear
as piece by piece it fell in place
all painted by Your brush.

ARLENE GAY LEVINE

Thanks to the Sun

Dear old Goldenface
we praise you
for your beaming light
for the smile of your early rises
for your laughter over the noon
for your goodnight grin

Be sure to come back tomorrow

JAMES BROUGHTON

Praise

I praise the sun
that lifts my eyes.

I praise the day
that sunlight brings.

I praise the light
that lets me read.

I praise the dark
that brings me sleep.

I praise the stars
that burn so bright.

I praise the night
when angels sing.

I lift this song
to heaven's high.

I sing this song
to praise the light.

PETER MARKUS

Father, We Thank Thee
(excerpt)

For this new morning with its light
   Father, we thank thee,
For rest and shelter of the night,
   Father, we thank thee,
For health and food, for love and friends,
For everything thy goodness sends,
Father in heaven, we thank thee.

RALPH WALDO EMERSON
(1803–1882)

A Path to Travel

Thank you, God, Source of all Being
Who blesses me this day
With truth and traditions,
Teachings and teachers,
A path to travel,
And the courage to walk it.

RABBI RAMI M. SHAPIRO

Morning Prayer

Now another day is breaking,
Sleep was sweet but so is waking.
Dear Lord, I promised you last night
Never again to sulk or fight.
Such vows are easier to keep
When a child is sound asleep.
Today, O Lord, for your dear sake,
I'll try to keep them when awake.

OGDEN NASH
(1902–1971)

20

i thank You God for most this amazing
(excerpt)

i thank You God for most this amazing
day:for the leaping greenly spirits of trees
and a blue true dream of sky;and for everything
which is natural which is infinite which is yes

E. E. CUMMINGS
(1894–1962)

MEALTIME
PRAYERS AND POEMS

Breakfast Prayer

Thank you, Lord, for wheat and corn,
Crunchy flakes are these,
Pour on milk and honey sweet,
Thanks for cows and bees.

The citrus tree that grows and gives
The juice that's in my glass,
Thank you for warm rain and sun,
The plump round fruit to bless.

Bless this breakfast, then, dear Lord,
Bless all who work to grow,
The corn and wheat, the cows and bees,
Thy faithful love to show.

VIRGINIA RYAN

23

The Johnny Appleseed Song

Oh, the Lord is good to me,
And so I thank the Lord,
For giving me the things I need:
The sun, the rain and the appleseed:
The Lord is good to me.

ATTRIBUTED TO JOHNNY APPLESEED
(JOHN CHAPMAN) (1774–1845)

Peanut Butter Prayer

Thank you God for peanut butter;
Thank you God for jelly.
And thank you for the way
They make me feel good in my belly!

DAVID FILLINGIM

Please Help Those with Less to Eat
(adapted)

Fruits and nuts and berries,
Growing ripe and sweet,
Vegetables and golden corn
All for us to eat.

Rich food in its plenty,
Picked and stored away,
While others in their countries
Are starving every day.

Mothers in the market,
Choosing what to eat,
Perhaps a rich fruit pudding
For a special treat.

In heats of other countries,
Little grows on land.
A mother looks at the food for the day
Which only fills one hand.

In lands of drought and hunger
No more, dear Lord, we pray
Will mothers ask the question
Which child to feed today?

JAMES ANTHONY CAREY
AGE 10

A Lunchtime Grace

Dear God,
Please help all the neglected people in the world who can't just go into the kitchen and get a sandwich.

A CHILD'S PRAYER FROM AUSTRALIA

Today

Today is very special;
it will never come again.
A red rose blooming,
that smile on Mother's face,
the apple pie she baked for us . . .
For all these,
I say grace.

ARLENE GAY LEVINE

29

Birthday Grace

Dear God,

Before I make a wish
And blow out the candles
I'll take a moment
To admire my cake and
To look at the faces
Around me.
Thank you for family,
And thank you for friends,
Thank you for cakes
With plenty of frosting,
And for one more candle
Every year.

Amen.

BARBARA YOUNGER

Traditional Jewish Toast

(Children can lead the toast with a glass of juice.)

To Life!

לְחַיִּים !

(le-KHAH-yeem)

AUTHOR UNKNOWN

BEDTIME
PRAYERS AND POEMS

My Flashlight

I take this light
Into the night, Lord,
To guide my way.
Help me to see
Down all dark paths
And let me carry
Your light with me
Wherever I go.

Amen.

BARBARA YOUNGER

But Not the Bugs That Bite

Dear God,

Thank you for the sun and moon
And all the stars at night.
Thank you for the fireflies
(But not the bugs that bite).

Thank you for the grass that's green
And trees where I can hide.
Thank you for the garden hose.
(I must go play outside.)

Thank you for my ABCs.
Learning them is fun.
Thank you for the school I'm in,
(And when the day is done).

Thank you for my family
And all my friends I know.
Thank you, God, for everyone.
(Now I've got to go.)

JEAN CAPEN TWEED

Dreams

Thunderstorms and dogs with wings,
Lots of silly no name things,
Blowing bubbles in the breeze,
Feeding lions nuts and cheese,
Roads that don't go anywhere,
Purple trees, a hungry bear—
Sometimes, when my dreams are bad,
I wake up feeling scared or sad.
"Thank you, God," I always say,
"For making bad dreams go away."

MARY RYER

A Child's Prayer

O heavenly Father, protect and bless
all things that have breath; guard them from
all evil, and let them sleep in peace.

ALBERT SCHWEITZER
(1875–1965)

36

Listen

Angels kiss
with wing-ed wisps
and speak to me
and speak to you.
Sh-h.

SHARON ANN REICH-GRAY

Before I Sleep

Before my mother dims the light
    I want to tell You why
I love the special things You made—
    The birds, the trees, the sky.

I love Your flowers in the Spring,
    The tulips pink and red
And crocuses that dare to bloom
    In a chilly garden bed.

I thank You for the summer sun
    That shines so warm and bright;
And for the golden moon I see
    Above me in the night.

I thank You for the autumn leaves
    Of red and gold in Fall,
For orange pumpkins fat and round
    And cornstalks straight and tall.

I won't forget the ice and snow
    You send on winter days.
The drifts of white, so soft and new,
    All seem to sing Your praise.

Yes, all the lovely things You made
    Are special, God, I know.
Before I close my eyes and sleep,
    I want to tell You so.

JEAN CONDER SOULE

For Goodness' Sake!

Now I lay me down to sleep.
I pray the Lord my soul to keep.
If I should die before I wake—

I hope I don't, for goodness' sake!

RICHARD NOCKLEBY
AGE 5

Forever

Be thou a bright flame before me,
Be thou a guiding star above me,
Be thou a smooth path below me,
Be thou a kindly shepherd behind me,
Today—tonight—and forever.

ST. COLUMBA OF IONA
(521–597)

ANYTIME
PRAYERS AND POEMS

My Question

Where are you, God?
  Up near a star,
Close to the sun,
  Is that where you are?

Where are you, God?
  Down close by me,
In the green grass,
  Or a small yellow bee?

In waving trees,
  Flying with birds,
Or can you be in
  My mother's kind words?

Where are you, God?
  Please can you tell?
I feel that I already
  Know you so well.

BARBARA STEINER

Prayer Places

Dear God,

I've found lots of
Good places to pray:
The woods, the swing,
My room on a rainy day,
A tent made out of sheets,
A fort built with leaves,
A garden wall,
A pine tree tall.
Almost every single day,
I find a new place to pray!

Amen.

BARBARA YOUNGER

If

Dear God, if from an acorn,
You'll build a mighty tree,
I get excited thinking
What You will help *me* be!

BONNIE COMPTON HANSON

My Happy Hamster

Dear Lord,
Please make sure my hamster is happy.
As he can't talk to me I can't be sure.
Also, please help me to look after him
better—I keep forgetting.

LOIS POTTER
AGE 11

Giving Thanks
Giving Thanks

giving thanks   giving thanks
for rain and rainbows
sun and sunsets
cats and catbirds
larks and larkspur

giving thanks   giving thanks
for cows and cowslips
eggs and eggplants
stars and starlings
dogs and dogwood

giving thanks   giving thanks
for watercress on river banks
for necks and elbows knees and shanks
for towers basins pools and tanks
for pumps and handles lifts and cranks

giving thanks   giving thanks
for ropes and coils and braids and hanks
for jobs and jokes and plots and pranks
for whistles bells and plinks and clanks
giving giving giving THANKS

EVE MERRIAM
(1916–1992)

A Traditional Prayer

Please give me what I ask, dear Lord,
If you'd be glad about it,
But if you think it's not for me,
Please help me do without it.

AUTHOR UNKNOWN

A Fair and Happy Game

Dear Lord,
Please help everyone
    who plays sports.
Help them to have
    good sportsmanship
    and a fair and happy game.
Please help the losing team
    not be grouchy.

ERIC HARDER
AGE 9

Wasps and Other Wonders

Dear God,

I don't mean to
Hurt your feelings,
But I don't see
Much use
For wasps
Or thornbushes
Or thunder
Or poison ivy.
But since you are God
And I'm just a kid
I like to think that
Wasps and
Other wonders
Are here for a reason
And you know
Just what
That reason is!

Amen.

BARBARA YOUNGER

Wings to Fly

Here I am in a wheelchair, God,
But you make me feel like a bird.
My feet are still, but you give my heart
Wings to fly when I'm afraid.

Thank you for friends and family,
Who smile and laugh and play with me.
Let them forget my wheelchair, God,
And love me just the way You do!

MARION SCHOEBERLEIN

Dolphin Prayer

Oh, God, you know
Sometimes I have
Trouble walking and
Talking
But today
I imagined
Riding on the back
Of a dolphin
Gliding through the
Water on a
Rainbow of
Bubbles.
Thank you.

ADDIE MEYER SANDERS

My Piggy Bank

Dear God,

My bank rattles
With the happy
Sound of the quarters
And nickels and dimes
I have saved.
When it's time
To spend them,
Remind me to share,
Help me to care,
About giving
And living
In a world where
There's lots to be done
To help everyone.

Amen.

BARBARA YOUNGER

Protect Me, O Lord

Protect me, O Lord;
My boat is so small,
And your sea is so big.

AUTHOR UNKNOWN
ANCIENT BRETON PRAYER

Friendship

Since we moved here, God,
You're the only friend I've got
which is okay, I guess—
or maybe not. I mean,
I sure would like to have a buddy my own size.
I bet You know that, though,
since Mama says You're wise.
Could You give me a new friend?
Someone with a basketball?
You and me will still be friends and all,
But right now,
I need somebody who'll invite me out to play.
Is that okay?

NIKKI GRIMES

Bless with Tenderness

Dear Father, hear and bless
Thy beasts and singing birds;
And guard with tenderness
Small things that have no words.

MARGARET WISE BROWN
(1910–1952)

I Believe

I believe in the sun even when it does not shine
I believe in love even when I do not feel it
I believe in God even when He is silent.

AUTHOR UNKNOWN

You and Me Together

O Lord, help me to understand
that You ain't going to let nothing
come my way that
You and me together
can't handle.

ANONYMOUS AFRICAN BOY

Harmony

May all I say and all I think
be in harmony with thee,
God within me, God beyond me,
maker of the trees.

CHINOOK PSALTER

Title and Author Index

Before I Sleep *(Jean Conder Soule)*   38

Birthday Grace *(Barbara Younger)*   30

Bless with Tenderness *(Margaret Wise Brown)*   55

Breakfast Prayer *(Virginia Ryan)*   23

But Not the Bugs That Bite *(Jean Capen Tweed)*   34

Child's Prayer, A *(Albert Schweitzer)*   36

Creation *(Arlene Gay Levine)*   15

Dolphin Prayer *(Addie Meyer Sanders)*   51

Dreams *(Mary Ryer)*   35

Fair and Happy Game, A *(Eric Harder)*   48

Father, We Thank Thee *(Ralph Waldo Emerson)*   18

Forever *(St. Columba of Iona)*   41

For Goodness' Sake! *(Richard Nockleby)*   40

Friendship *(Nikki Grimes)*   54

Giving Thanks   Giving Thanks *(Eve Merriam)*   46

Harmony *(Author unknown)*   57

I Believe *(Author unknown)*   55

If *(Bonnie Compton Hanson)*   45

i thank You God for most this amazing
   (E. E. Cummings)   21

Johnny Appleseed Song, The *(John Chapman)*   24

Listen *(Sharon Ann Reich-Gray)*   37

Lunchtime Grace, A *(Author unknown)*   28

Morning *(Madeleine L'Engle)*   11

Morning Has Broken *(Eleanor Farjeon)*   12

Morning Prayer *(Ogden Nash)*   20

My Flashlight *(Barbara Younger)*   33

My Happy Hamster *(Lois Potter)*   45

My Piggy Bank *(Barbara Younger)*   52

My Question *(Barbara Steiner)*   43

Path to Travel, A *(Rabbi Rami M. Shapiro)*   19

Peanut Butter Prayer *(David Fillingim)*   25

Please Help Those with Less to Eat
  (James Anthony Carey)   26

Praise *(Peter Markus)*   17

Prayer Places *(Barbara Younger)*   44

Protect Me, O Lord *(Author unknown)*   53

Song *(Robert Browning)*   14

Thanks to the Sun *(James Broughton)*   16

Today *(Arlene Gay Levine)*   29

Traditional Jewish Toast *(Author unknown)*   31

Traditional Prayer, A *(Author unknown)*   48

Wasps and Other Wonders *(Barbara Younger)*   49

Wings to Fly *(Marion Schoeberlein)*   50

You and Me Together *(Author unknown)*   56

Acknowledgments

Grateful acknowledgment is made to the authors and publishers for the use of the following material. Every effort has been made to contact original sources. If notified, the publisher will rectify an omission in future editions. • James Broughton for "Thanks to the Sun." • Cook Communications Ministries for "Please Help Those with Less to Eat" by James Anthony Carey, "Lunchtime Grace" (author unknown), and "My Happy Hamster" by Lois Potter from *365 Children's Prayers* by Carol Watson, copyright © 1989 by Cook Communications Ministries. Reprinted with permission of Chariot Victor Publishing, a division of Cook Communications Ministries. May not be further reproduced. All rights reserved. • Curtis Brown Ltd. for "Morning Prayer" by Ogden Nash. Copyright © 1961 by Ogden Nash. Reprinted by permission of Curtis Brown, Ltd. • David Fillingim for "Peanut Butter Prayer." • Bonnie Compton Hanson for "If." • Eric Harder for "A Fair and Happy Game." • Harold Ober Associates Incorporated for "Morning Has Broken" by Eleanor Farjeon. Copyright © 1931 by Eleanor Farjeon. Reprinted with permission of Harold Ober Associates Incorporated. • HarperCollins Publishers for "Bless with Tenderness" by Margaret Wise Brown from *A Child's Good Night Book* by Margaret Wise Brown, copyright © 1943, 1950 by Margaret Wise Brown, copyright renewed 1978 by Roberta B. Rauch. • Just Us Books for "Friendship" by Nikki Grimes from *A Child's Heart* by Nikki Grimes. Copyright © 1993 by Just Us Books and Nikki Grimes. Reprinted by permission of Just Us Books. • Lescher & Lescher, Ltd., for "Morning" by Madeleine L'Engle from *Everyday Prayers* by Madeleine L'Engle, copyright © 1974 by Madeleine L'Engle. Reprinted by permission of Lescher & Lescher, Ltd. • Arlene Gay Levine for "Creation" and "Today." • Liveright Publishing Corporation for the lines from "i thank You God for most this amazing," copyright © 1950, 1978, 1991 by the Trustees for the E. E. Cummings Trust. Copyright © 1979 by George James Firmage, from *Complete Poems: 1904-1962* by E. E. Cummings, edited by George J. Firmage. Reprinted by permission of Liveright Publishing Corporation. • Peter Markus for "Praise." • Rhena Schweitzer Miller for "A Child's Prayer" by Albert Schweitzer. • Thomas Nelson, Inc., for "A Traditional Prayer" from *Classic Children's Prayers* by Alan and Linda Parry. Copyright © 1995 by Hunt & Thorpe. Published in the U.S.A. by Tommy Nelson™, a division of Thomas Nelson, Inc. • Lenora Nockleby for "For Goodness' Sake!" • Sharon Ann Reich-Gray for "Listen." • Marian Reiner for "Giving Thanks Giving Thanks" by Eve Merriam from *Fresh Paint* by Eve Merriam. Copyright © 1986 by Eve Merriam. Reprinted by permission of Marian Reiner. • Virginia Ryan for "Breakfast Prayer." • Mary Ryer for "Dreams." • Addie Meyer Sanders for "Dolphin Prayer." • Marion Schoeberlein for "Wings to Fly." • Rabbi Rami M. Shapiro for "A Path to Travel." • Jean Conder Soule for "Before I Sleep." • Barbara Steiner for "My Question." • Jean Capen Tweed for "But Not the Bugs That Bite." • Barbara Younger for "Birthday Grace," "My Flashlight," "My Piggy Bank," "Prayer Places," and "Wasps and Other Wonders." • *Permissions compiled by Tricia Treacy.*